THE DOLMENS
OF JERSEY

A guide to the major Neolithic stone monuments
in Jersey and what we know of the people who built them

by Peter Hunt

Edited by Ralph Nichols, John Renouf and Doug Ford

Photographs on pages 5, 13, 17, 18, 20, 26, 35, 36 and 45 by Gareth
Syvret. Other photographs courtesy of the Société Jersiaise or the
Jersey Museums Service. Illustrations by Gill Kay. Watercolours by
Ursula Hare. Map references and reproductions on pages 27 and 31
with kind permission of Perry's Guide to Jersey

Table of Contents

The Dolmens of Jersey

WELCOME to this guide to the Neolithic stone monuments and archaeological sites of the Island of Jersey.

This guide is an introduction to the Neolithic (new stone) sites on the Island. The artefacts which were excavated from the sites may be found on display at La Hougue Bie, Grouville, and the Jersey Museum in St Helier. Further information on the dolmens and menhirs can be found at the Lord Coutanche Library of the Société Jersiaise at 7 Pier Road, St Helier, or at the Jersey Museum, St Helier.

The guide is in four sections with a map on the centre pages. There is an introduction, there are three different tour routes, a brief description of each site and, finally, more information on Neolithic people, their way of life and death.

It is worth noting that some of the sites are not easily accessible. You must be prepared to find parking nearby and to walk to each site, in some cases through woodland. Suitable shoes and clothing are recommended.

How it all Began

IT is generally agreed that sometime about or soon after 5000 BC the rising sea had separated the Channel Islands from the mainland of France. At about the same time, the way of life of early man changed from that of hunter/gatherers to that of farmers cultivating grain and domesticating wild animals. This farming society has been classified by archaeologists as the Neolithic Age.

To these Neolithic people of adjacent France, the islands would have presented a similar and attractive environment. Jersey was heavily wooded and more extensive than now since large areas, tidal at present, had not been overwhelmed by the rising sea level of post glacial times. Possibly the early Neolithic settlements were established at the west, south, and east in the Island.

The settlers would have established their bases on the coast and would have worked their way into the woodlands to hunt and to increase their farm lands. There is no evidence of a true settlement in the Island or anywhere else in adjacent parts of France at present. The Pinnacle site (Le Pinacle) in St Ouen had hearths but it is thought to be a stone axe producing site. Neolithic people passed by and visited Green Island (La Motte) in St Clement and, in so doing, left middens of shells to reveal their presence.

The time span covering the Neolithic and early Bronze Age in Jersey was some 3000 years. There is evidence to indicate that two major movements of people and/or ideas were originally involved: one coming from the heart of Europe via the Danube and Rhone river valleys, the other up from the Mediterranean through France and along the Atlantic coasts.

It was this latter group, from the south, who became involved in the megalithic tradition and introduced the earliest of our stone monuments, those known as passage graves — so named because the main chamber was reached by a narrow entrance and passage way.

The main examples of Passage Graves are La Sergenté, Les Monts Grantez, Le Mont Ubé, La Pouquelaye de Faldouet, Le Mont de la

Le Pinacle, St Ouen

Ville (transferred and rebuilt in Henley-on-Thames in England in 1788) and the finest of them all — La Hougue Bie. It is now accepted that the monuments remained in use for over 2000 years and were obviously far more important than just burial places.

They must have been centres of worship, community centres, even territorial markers and centres of civic and religious power. The tradition of significant stone structures continued but changed over a period of time. In the later Neolithic, the simpler Gallery Grave or *allée couverte* as they are known regionally, was developed. The best examples of this style are at La Ville ès Nouaux and Le Couperon.

By the beginning of the second Millennium BC, styles of burial changed again, becoming even simpler. This third type is known as the Cist-in-Circle style monument which featured a central stone or Cist set in a circle of outer stones.

The best examples of this style are at La Hougue des Platons and the northerly grave at La Ville ès Nouaux, this site being the only one found so far where two different styles of monuments are in the same place.

The Neolithic People

THE Neolithic way of life developed slowly and occurred in different places at different times, progressing westwards and eastwards from the Middle East over centuries. Nonetheless, it was a true revolution after which human kind would never be the same again.

We can never be sure exactly how the Neolithic people led their lives but there is enough archaeological data for us to make an informed guess.

The major innovation was raising crops instead of just hunting and gathering. This development allowed, indeed forced, the creation of permanent settlements needed to tend and harvest crops. Early styles of buildings vary according to location and the building materials available. In our area, they were most certainly made from wood, although no trace of a period building has yet been found.

There is little doubt that skills in construction and in the creation of the tools for farming and mining developed during this period as well as pottery for domestic use. One major reason was that food could be better harvested and that artisans skilled in manufacture could concentrate on their tasks rather than concentrating on survival alone.

In these early times, until the beginning of the Bronze Age, the majority of the communities would have lived at relative peace; farming, hunting, fishing and trading; defences being built against wild animals rather than against fellow humans.

It is also probable that there was a traditional division of labour between the men and the women although at times both sexes would be involved in harvesting and major building works. Men would undertake the tasks of herding, mining, axe-making, tree-felling, hunting, fishing and building whereas the women raised the children, spun and weaved, cultivated the soil, grew the crops and fired the pottery.

We can only imagine how immediate life must have been. In spite of their newly-found means of food production, allowing permanent settlements, the lives of the Neolithic people were still close to nature and dependent on the natural cycles of the seasons.

Drawing: GILL KAY

**Representation of the 'Iceman' found in the
Tyrolean Alps in 1991**

Why the Neolithic peoples of the Atlantic seaboard moved to the construction of major monuments in stone can only be guessed at. It is possible that a veneration for stone was present among the native people at the time when the Neolithic culture arrived. Or that either or both felt an affinity to the strong granite rocks of the coast. Who knows! Whatever the reason, the stone monument became the defining attribute of the Neolithic in our area and clearly represented a focus of religious belief.

Hougue des Géonnais Dolmen, St Ouen, 1929

The Tours

WHICHEVER tour you choose, it is highly recommended that your final stop is made at La Hougue Bie, a site recognised for its importance throughout Europe and where there is an archaeological gallery.

Dolmens are an invaluable part of our heritage. Please ensure that they are treated with care and respect at all times.

Drawing: GILL KAY

Representation of a Neolithic village

There are three tours you may wish to follow

Tour 1 is a full tour of all the dolmens with access to the public and includes the major menhirs and Neolithic sites. You should allow a day to complete the tour.

Tour 2 is a short tour which will introduce you to the three types of dolmens and is limited to the east of the island. You should allow half a day to complete the tour.

Tour 3 is a medium length tour which will introduce you to all the major dolmens but not to the menhirs and other Neolithic sites.

You should allow a day for this tour in order to take the opportunity to visit Hamptonne and Gorey Castle as well as the monuments. On this tour, you will circle the Island.

Replica of a Neolithic house, La Hougue Bie

Dr Mark Patton re-excavating La Hougue des Geonnais in 1990

1. Full tour of major sites — by Parish

THIS is a full day's tour of all the monuments with public access and includes the major menhirs and Neolithic sites. The site references are given from Perry's official guide to Jersey though you should be able to find the sites comfortably from the instructions given for each site.

St Helier

La Ville ès Nouaux
Gallery Grave and Cist-in-Circle   **p 39   H4 ●**

PROCEED from St Helier on the A1, La Route de St Aubin, (the Inner Road). At First Tower, turn right up Le Mont Cochon. On your left is St Andrew's Church. The dolmens are in the park to the west of the church. To park, take the next left, La Rue de Trachy, where there are several parking spaces at the side of the road.

Cist-in-Circle dolmen de la Ville ès Nouaux

● For map references refer to Perry's Guide to Jersey

St Brelade

La Sergenté
Passage Grave **p 46 D3**

Les Blanches Banques
Ossuary and Menhirs **p 35 G4**

TO find La Sergenté, drive west along La Route Orange. Turn right toward La Pulente at La Rue de Sergenté. Opposite the entrance to the Atlantic Hotel, turn left into La Parcq de L'Oeillière. Follow the road round, bear left then right onto the headland. Follow the dirt road round to your left and the monument is on your right. Return to La Rue de Sergenté, turn left and drive down to the La Grande Route des Mielles (the Five Mile Road). Opposite the Le Braye café, turn right along Le Chemin des Basses Mielles. There is a car park on your right. Walk inland, towards the golf club on top of the hills and you will find the menhirs and ossuary.

La Sergenté dolmen, St Brelade

13

St Ouen

Les Monts Grantez
Passage Grave **p 15 F4**

Le Pinacle
Neolithic site and Gallo-Roman shrine **p 6 A4**

La Hougue des Geonnais
Passage grave **p 7 H3**

DRIVE North along the La Grande Route des Mielles following the road inland and up the hill (Le Mont Pinel).

At the cluster of houses on your right near the top of the hill, turn right along the La Rue de Grantez. A sign to the dolmen will be on the wall of a farm house on your right about a quarter of a mile along the road.

Turn right into Le Chemin des Monts, and follow the road to the car park at the end. The dolmen is in a field to the left of Le Chemin des Monts, a short walk away.

Le Pinacle is in the area of the race course at the north-west tip of the Island. From St Ouen, travel west along La Route de Vinchelez (B55). Pass the turn to Grosnez Castle and the race course, on your right. After half a mile, on your right-hand side, will be a car track. Turn right along the track, bearing left at the end. Park by the model aircraft tarmac strip. Walk west towards the sea. You will find the outcrop of Le Pinacle and can descend to the Neolithic site and Gallo-Roman shrine.

Return to the main road and retrace your route, passing the Portinfer tea rooms on your right and the sign to Plémont on your left. Take the second small road to your left, La Rue des Geonnais. After a quarter of a mile, you will see a cluster of houses and a narrow turn to the left. The dolmen is a little further on your right. There is room for maybe two cars to park on the right.

Les Montes Grantez dolmen, St Ouen

Hamptonne House, part of the Hamptonne complex

● *Stop off at Hamptonne, Jersey's Country Life Museum, St Lawrence*   p 29 F1

HAMPTONNE is well worth a visit, both for refreshment and to see the country museum. Allow an hour at least. From St Ouen travel through St Mary to St John. Having passed St John's church, take the major road right, the A10 towards St Lawrence.

Drive through Carréfour Selous and, after three quarters of a mile look out for a small turn on your left just before the Shell garage. Turn sharp left almost back on yourself.

This is La Rue des Corvées. Follow the signs to Hamptonne. If you reach St Lawrence's church on your right you have over-shot your destination. Turn back and you will find that Hamptonne is clearly sign-posted.

Cist-in-Circle dolmen at La Hougue des Platons

Trinity

La Hougue des Platons

Cist-in-Circle   **p 13 F4**

LA Hougue des Platons is close to the highest point on the Island (149m). From Hamptonne return to St John. Turn right along the main road, La Route des Issues, to the cross roads at Les Hautes Croix. Turn left along La Rue du Betchet ès Cats to the T-junction. Turn right along La Rue des Platons (C97). After half a mile, you will see the BBC transmitter mast. Once you have passed the mast, take the next turning left, La Rue d'Egypte. The dolmen is now above you on your left. Parking is difficult although you can park at a small lay-by on your left. Walk up to the dolmen.

La Pouquelaye de Faldouet dolmen

St Martin

Le Couperon
Gallery Grave   **p 24 B3**

La Pouquelaye de Faldouet
Passage Grave   **p 44 C2**

FROM La Hougue des Platons, retrace your route to the main road and drive to Trinity church. Continue east on the B31 towards St Martin. Having passed the Zoo continue straight on for a mile and a quarter and bear left on B38, La Grande Route de Rozel. Take the first right, the B91, La Rue des Pelles. After half a mile, the B91 turns sharp right. At this turn, take the small road turning left. Keep straight on down to the sea. The dolmen, Le Couperon, is at the bottom to the left of the car park.

Return to the B91 and follow the road to St Martin, keeping on the Grande Route de Faldouet until you reach Ransom's Garden Centre. Bear left. You will quickly come upon a small road on your left, La Rue de la Pouclée et Des Quatres Chemins. Turn into it. After about half a mile turn left into Le Mont Mallet. The dolmen is on your left in the trees. You will have to find parking nearby and follow the indicated path to the dolmen.

● *Stop off at Mont Orgueil Castle, Gorey* p 44 D3

Mont Orgueil, Gorey

Return to La Rue de la Pouclée et des Quartes Chemins and turn left. This will bring you down to the B29. Turn right and follow the signs to Gorey Castle and Harbour.

St Clement

La Motte (Green Island)
Site   **p 56 B5**
Le Mont Ubé
Passage Grave   **p56 C 1**

La Motte, or Green Island, St Clement

DRIVE along the Bay of Grouville, keeping the golf course on your left and continue along the coast road, the A4. After a few miles, you will see the Shakespeare Hotel on your right. Half a mile further on is a road to a car park on your left. Park and visit La Motte (Green Island).

Return to the main coast road and cross over to La Rue de Samarès. Drive straight along it, cross the major road (A5) and continue up La Rue de la Blinerie.

The path to the Le Mont Ubé dolmen is under a quarter of a mile on the right. Park as close as you can to the edge of the road and take the path to the dolmen.

Le Mont Ubé dolmen, St Clement

21

Grouville

La Hougue Bie Passage Grave   **p42 D31**

FOLLOW La Rue de Blinerie and turn right into La Rue du Coin. Follow this little road until you meet the major A3 road, La Rue a Don. Turn right along the A3 for just over half a mile. Turn sharp left into la Rue du Boulivot, passing the Grouville Arsenal on your left. Follow the B46 inland along La Route de la Francheville until you arrive at La Hougue Bie. You will now have completed the tour. The staff at La Hougue Bie will be happy to give you directions for your return to base.

The Mont de la Ville dolmen, now in Henley-on-Thames, Oxfordshire

2. short tour

THIS short tour covers the three major types of dolmens. It will take about half a day and covers the east, north and north east of the island.

St Clement
Le Mont Ubé Passage Grave **p 56 C1**

St Martin
La Pouquelaye de Faldouet Passage Grave **p 44 C2**
Le Couperon Gallery Grave **p 24 B3**

Trinity
La Hougue des Platons Cist-in-Circle **p 13 F4**

Grouville
La Hougue Bie Passage Grave **p 42 D3**

LEAVE St Helier heading east on the A5, La Grande Route de St Clement. Pass the Samarès Manor and Farm and take the next left, La Rue de la Blinerie. The Le Mont Ubé dolmen is in the woods a quarter of a mile up on the right. Park with care and climb up the path.

Continue along La Rue de la Blinerie until you meet a small country road on your right, La Rue du Coin. Follow this little road till you meet the major A3 road, La Rue à Don. Turn right along the A3 and travel to Gorey.

If you feel that you have time stop off at
Le Mont Orgueil Castle, Gorey

LEAVE Gorey on the B30 turning sharp right on the B29 towards Anne Port. Follow the road round turning left into Les Charrières D'Anne Port. You will pass the Anne Port Hotel on your left.

1. Le Pinacle
2. Les Monts de Grantez
3. La Hougue des Géonnais
4. La Hougue Bie

5. Ville ès Nouaux
6. La Sergenté
7. La Hougue des Platons
8. La Pouquelaye de Faldouët

RIBUTION OF MONUMENT SITES

Department of Planning and Environment
f the Men of the Trees

7

Trinity

10

St Martin

Gorey

La Haye Bie

St Helier

4

St Saviour

5

Grouville

KM 1 2
MILES 1

9

St Clement

13

). Mont Ubé

10. Le Couperon

1. The Ossuary

2. Les Blanches Banques Menhirs

13. La Motte or Green Island

Ascend the hill and take the first left towards Le Mont Mallet. The dolmen de Faldouet is on your right off Le Mont Mallet. Continue to the T-junction, turn left and descend to the B29. Turn left. Pass Anne Port and through St Catherine's Bay. Follow round the one-way system. Do not turn right on the

Le Couperon dolmen, St Martin

road that leads to St Catherine's breakwater. Once you have turned back on yourself in the one way system, you will come to a sharp right turn, the B91, La Rue du Villot. At the summit, you will come to La Haie Fleurie Equestrian Centre. The B91 bears left. Go straight across and down the little road, La Rue du Scez. The Couperon dolmen is at the bottom to the left of the car park.

Return to the B91 and turn right, La Rue des Pelles. Turn left at the T-junction and bear right onto the B31. Continue into Trinity. Turn right at Trinity church, then left, keeping the church on your left and then turn right on the C97, La Rue du Tas de Geon. At the T-junction, turn left on the C97, La Rue des Platons, and take the next right, La Rue D'Egypte. La Hougue des Platons dolmen is on the top of the hill on your left. Park in the small lay-by and walk up to the dolmen.

Return to Trinity church. Keeping the church on your right, turn left onto the B31, La Rue ès Picots. Having passed the Zoo, keep straight on towards Maufant, the B46.

Do not take the B30 towards St Martin. The B46 will bring you to the A6, La Grande Route de St Martin. Turn right and immediately left into La Rue du Trot which will bring you to La Hougue Bie. The short tour ends at La Hougue Bie. The staff will be very happy to give you directions to your home base.

3. Longer tour

YOU should allow a day for this tour as the route circles the Island

St Clement
Le Mont Ubé Passage Grave **p 56 C1**

St Martin
La Pouquelaye de Faldouet Passage Grave **p 44 C2**
Le Couperon Gallery Grave **p 24 B3**

Trinity
La Hougue des Platons Cist-in-Circle **p 13 F4**

LEAVE St Helier heading east on the A5, La Grande Route de St Clement. Pass the Samarès Manor and Farm and take the next left, La Rue de la Blinerie. The Le Mont Ubé dolmen is in the woods a quarter of a mile up on the right.

Park with care and climb up the path. Continue along La Rue de la Blinerie until you meet a small country road on your right, La Rue du Coin. Follow this little road till you meet the major A3 road, La Rue à Don. Turn right along the A3 and then travel to Gorey.

Road map showing the Faldouet dolmen

If you have time, visit Mont Orgueil Castle

27

1920s excavation of the Couperon dolmen, St Martin

Leave Gorey on the B30 turning sharp right on the B29 towards Anne Port. Follow the road round turning left into Les Charrières D'Anne Port. You will pass the Anne Port Hotel on your left. Ascend the hill and take the first left towards Le Mont Mallet. The dolmen de Faldouet is on your right off Le Mont Mallet.

Continue to the T-junction, turn left and descend to the B29. Turn left. Pass Anne Port and through St Catherine's Bay. Follow round the one way system. Do not turn right, unless you wish to, on the road that leads to St Catherine's breakwater. Once you have turned back on yourself in the one way system, you will come to a sharp right turn, the B91, La Rue du Villot.

At the summit, you will come to La Haie Fleurie Equestrian Centre. The B91 bears left. Go straight across and down the little road, La Rue du Scez. The Couperon dolmen is at the bottom to the left of the car park.

Remains of the dolmen excavated in 1952 in the centre of St Helier

Return to the B91 and turn right, La Rue des Pelles. Turn left at the T-junction and bear right onto the B31.

Continue into Trinity. Turn right at Trinity church, then left, keeping the church on your left and then turn right on the C97, La Rue du Tas de Geon.

At the T-junction, turn left on the C97, La Rue des Platons and take the next right, La Rue D'Egypte. La Hougue des Platons dolmen is on the top of the hill on your left. Park in the small lay-by and walk up to the dolmen.

If you feel you have time Stop off at Hamptonne, Jersey's Country Life Museum, St Lawrence   **p 29 F1**

You should allow an hour at least to visit Hamptonne.

Return to the C97, La Rue des Platons, and turn right. Take the third left, after the viewing point on your right, the B63, La Rue du Betchet ès Cats to Hautes Croix. Turn right to St John, on the A9. You will come to Jersey Pearl on your right. Turn left and head south on the A10, La Rue de la Mare Bellam. Drive through Carréfour Selous and, after three quarters of a mile, look out for a small turn on your left which virtually brings you back on yourself. This is La Rue des Corvées. Follow the signs to Hamptonne. If you reach St

Excavating Les Monts Grantez, 1912

Road map showing the Hamptonne Museum (right) and (above) the cider press at Hamptonne

Lawrence's church on your right you have over-shot. Turn back and you will find that Hamptonne is clearly sign-posted. If you do not have time to visit Hamptonne, follow the directions as above but when you reach Jersey Pearl, do not turn left but carry straight on following the signs to St Ouen. Then follow the instructions in the next paragraph continuing from the T-junction in St Ouen.

31

St Ouen
Les Monts Grantez Passage Grave p 15   F4

St Brelade
La Sergenté Passage Grave   p 46   D3

St Helier
La Ville ès Nouaux Gallery Grave and Cist-in-Circle   p 29 H4

RETURN to the A10, turn right and head north. At Carréfour Selous, turn left on the B39 to St Mary. Follow the road to St Ouen. At the T-junction in St Ouen, (the Farmer's Inn pub will be on your left), turn right then left opposite the Parish Hall, the B64, La Route du Marais.

After half a mile, turn left down a small road, La Rue des Nouettes. After a quarter of a mile, turn right and cross over into Le Chemin des Monts. (There is a small right-left to achieve this manoeuvre). Proceed to the car park at the end. Les Monts Grantez dolmen is in a field on your left.

Return to the junction and turn left. Continue till you meet the major road, the B64, La Route du Marais, and turn left down to the sea. Follow La Grande Route des Mielles along the bay, pass La Pulente pub and climb up the hill. Near the top of the hill, you will see the entrance to the Atlantic hotel on your left. Turn right into Le Parcq de L'Oeillière. Follow round the one way system taking the exit left towards the headland. The La Sergenté dolmen is in the field to your left.

Return to the main road and turn right. At the T-junction, turn left and follow the signs to St Aubin and St Helier. At First Tower on the A2, Victoria Avenue, turn left and ascend Mont Cochon (B27). After a quarter of a mile, turn left into La Rue de Trachy. The dolmens are at the bottom of the park on your left, adjacent to the church.

Return to Mont Cochon and descend. Turn left, taking the A1 to St Helier. At the roundabout opposite the Grand Hotel, turn left and continue on the ring road, following the signs for Five Oaks and St Martin.

Interior of La Hougue Bie, 1924, before restoration

Grouville

La Hougue Bie Passage Grave

p 42   D3

At the roundabout at Five Oaks, turn right along the B28, Princes Tower Road. At the T-junction, turn left, the B46, La Rue du Trot. La Hougue Bie is on your left.

You have now completed this tour which will have introduced you not only to the major dolmens but also will have shown you many different aspects of Jersey's varied country, village and town life. The staff at La Hougue Bie will be happy to give you directions to return to your base.

About the Dolmens

PLEASE note these descriptions are brief. Further information on each site can be found at the Société Jersiaise, the Jersey Museum or at La Hougue Bie. Whichever tour you choose, please refer to this main list for descriptions of the site you have chosen to visit.

St Helier
La Ville ès Nouaux

There are two structures at this site, the earlier single gallery grave or *allée couverte* being to the south. The feature of this dolmen is that it is a rectangular chamber set within a ring of stones. The second structure was discovered in 1883. This is know as a 'Cist-in-Circle'. The outer circle of stones would have been supplemented by dry-stone packing. The inner cist, formed by two standing stones or orthostats, two boulders and a capstone, would have been covered by a mound of clay. The tomb was empty when excavated.
Probable date 2800 — 2300 BC

St Brelade
1. Les Blanches Banques Menhirs and Ossuary

The reason why our ancestors erected menhirs, (large, upright stones) is unknown — territory markers? Memorials? Star indicators? (The three at Les Blanches Banques do resemble the Belt of Orion.) Shrines? Time-pieces?
The three menhirs known as the Broken, the Great and the Little are of granite so were transported from elsewhere in the Island indicating that this was an important communal site. The Ossuary is ruined. What is left was restored after excavation in 1922 when bones identifying the presence of at least 20 individuals were found.
Probable date 2850 — 1500 BC

The gallery grave at La Ville ès Nouaux, St Helier

2. La Sergenté

This site, a small passage grave, is unique to the Channel Islands because the roof was corbelled. (Corbeling is the beehive shaping of a chamber by the in-stepping of the roofing stones). It can be compared to the corbelled tombs in Brittany, Normandy and Spain. Probable date 4500 — 4000 BC

La Hougue de Geonnais

St Ouen
1. Les Monts Grantez

This fine example of a passage grave lay originally under a low mound some 18 metres by 9 metres All the structural stones are of granite, most quarried locally though some stones are from the Corbière area in the south west. Bones found in the main chamber included those of six adults and a child as well as bones from cows, pigs, sheep, wild horse and deer. In a niche at the inner end of the passage, the skeleton of another adult was found arranged in a sitting position supported by a heap of stones.

Probable date 4000 — 3250 BC

2. Le Pinacle

This site is one of the most spectacular and important in Jersey and its usage can be traced through the Neolithic period to the Gallo-Roman times, there being the remains of a Neolithic grave and axe factory as well as of a Gallo-Roman forum. As always, there is confusion as to the real purpose of the site despite the finds of animal bones, axe-hammers, flint work and decorated fine-ware pottery. Its position between the higher plateau and the sea makes it an unlikely choice for a farming base. It is also vulnerable to attack from above so it is unlikely that it would have been chosen as a defensive position. It is pretty certain that stone axes were produced at the site but there is also an attractive theory that this was a open-air ritual site which made use of the dramatic west facing rock, Le Pinacle — a natural menhir.

Probable date first phase 4850 — 4250 BC,

Beaker phase 2850 — 2250 BC

3. La Hougue des Geonnais

Little is now to be seen of the original structure though the outline of the passage and the chamber is recognisable. When excavated in 1929, a circular rubble mound was found to enclose what seems to have been a substantial passage grave. The site is, however, worth a visit not only for the remains of this dolmen but also for its spectacular view over the north coast. It was recently re-excavated and certain standing stones have been replaced.

Probable date 4000 — 3250 BC

Trinity

La Hougue des Platons

The central cist formed by a capstone resting on three walls of laid slabs has been removed from the site and can be seen at La Hougue Bie. What remains is the mound, 8 metres in diameter and 1.5 metres high, enclosed by a circle of massive blocks of volcanic 'tuff' (a mixture of volcanic ash and other erupted materials).

Probable date 2850 — 2250 BC

Faldouet dolmen, looking west from an elevation of 18 ft

St Martin

1. Le Couperon

Despite considerable depredation, the form of the original dolmen is clear. It was a rectangular chamber built of conglomerate orthostats (single upright stones) and massive capstones. The whole would have been covered by a mound which in this case would have been rectangular as remains of a slab-built peristalith (small stone supporting wall) indicate its outer limits.

Probable date 2850 — 2250 BC

2. La Pouquelaye de Faldouet

This is one of the most intriguing sites in Jersey. It marks a development in the design of passage graves which culminated in the dolmen at Le Mont de la Ville (removed and reconstructed at Henley-on-Thames in 1788). The chamber, 14 metres in length, is enclosed by a circular mound made of small stones. The entrance passage leads to a circular area with four small cists around the sides though there were probably more originally. This is turn leads to the massive paved chamber the capstone of which weighs some 24 tonnes.

The visible height is misleading as the floor was raised in 1910. It is thought that neither the passage nor the central area were ever roofed. The present structure is a reconstruction in whole or in part so its original form remains suspect.

Probable date 4000 — 3250 BC

St Clement

1. Le Mont Ubé

Discovered by quarrymen in 1848, this dolmen whilst still impressive has been sadly damaged. The capstones have been destroyed, the contents disturbed and its mound scattered. The dolmen runs ESE to WNW, is just over 12 metres long and an arrangement of four chambers is to be found at the western end. The stones are both local diorite and granite brought from Le Hocq, 1 kilometre away.

Probable date 4000 — 3250 BC

2. Green Island (La Motte)

Green Island is likely to have been a peninsula until at least the early 1600s, but subsequent sea erosion created the island. It is still under threat as an island and plans are in hand to preserve what is left. It is thought to be one of the original centres of Neolithic settlement though no traces of habitation have been found. There are the

The chapel and mound at La Hougue Bie

remains of a cairn to the east and on a neck of land to the south east
the remains of a cemetery of at least eighteen slab-walled and roofed
cists (grave stones) sunk into the soil.

Probable date of first settlement 4000 BC

Grouville

La Hougue Bie

This magnificent passage grave was discovered by excavations undertaken by its owners, the Société Jersiaisé, in 1924. The tomb had lain concealed for some four thousand years though lack of finds within the tomb suggest that it may have been robbed in the past. However, its impressive mound and its emotive atmosphere must have been reason enough for the two chapels to have been erected on the mound during the Mediaeval period as well as making Christian a pagan site. The grave is in the shape of a cross, the entrance passage leading to the main chamber which has three cells adjoining it to the north, west and east.

It is the only dolmen in the Channel Islands to have a cell at the western end of the main chamber though a similar format has been found at New Grange in Ireland, at Maes Howe in Orkney and at Gavr'lnis in Brittany. The workmanship of the tomb is of the highest quality. There is little doubt that the structural stones were chosen for their shape and smoothness and the drystone walling between the supporting stones was occasionally laid to ensure that the roof had a constant height. Even the floor had been paved with a layer of beach pebbles. The stones themselves would have to have been transported from their quarries to the south, south west and south east of the site at a distance of no less that 3.5 kilometres — a not inconsiderable task in itself.

The mound was made from loose stone and rubble, quarried from more accessible areas to the west and east of the mound. Surprisingly, relatively few artefacts were found within the tomb which is why robbery is suspected at some stage in its history. There were bones of some eight adults, both male and female, and of various animals, flint arrowheads and shards of pottery. The most important find was a massive quern (a stone handmill for corn) which had been deliberately buried under the transverse slab at the entrance to the end chamber. The tomb was sealed on purpose and the entrance covered over. Why will probably always remain a mystery.

Probable date 4000 — 3250 BC

Building the Dolmens

IT is highly unlikely that we will ever know exactly why and how the monuments were built, how long they took to build or, indeed, what were their true functions other than as graves or even calendars. However, we can make a pretty good guess.

First the stone had to be collected or quarried. From stone or megalithic (the Greek word for large stones) graves around the world, it is known that our early ancestors had the skills to work with stone. They would find the weak lines in the stone, insert a wooden drill or wedge till the stone cracked. It is also thought that they knew how to crack stone by the use of fire and water.

The stones then had to be transported to the site. This would be done by man power pulling the stones, probably over wooden rollers, with ropes made from animal hide or tree bark.

It should be remembered that our concept of time would have been quite alien to our Neolithic ancestors. They would not have been subject as we are to the Clock. They would have accepted that a task had to be done and manage their lives around that task — taking as long as necessary to complete it, with intervals away from the task as need be. There is no doubt, however, about their ingenuity as builders. Once it is realised how the dolmens were built there is a logical simplicity about the method. First, a pit would be dug to the required size, the top of the pit being where the capstones or roofing stones were to be placed.

The wall stones would be pulled to the edge and over it — leaving the centre of balance on the earth. Depending on the size of the stones to be moved, there are two methods they could have employed. For very large stones such as at Stonehenge, there is a theory that they may have used A-frames to help. For smaller stones, they would have pulled them over the edge to settle into a recess in the ground made to receive them. They might then be secured with stone fragments. For larger stones, a second stone would be placed on the wall stone and as the smaller stone was

The restored interior of La Hougue Bie

pulled forward, its weight would tip the wall stone into its recess.

When all the wall stones were in place, the grave would be refilled with the earth. The capstones could then be pulled into place across the roof of the filled grave. When that task had been completed, the earth would be again dug out and the grave was ready for use, the earth being finally used as a mound to the grave.

Simple but very ingenious.

It is thought that menhirs, the single large stones that stand upright, would have been placed using the same method. Why they were placed where they were will probably always remain a mystery. There are countless theories — territory markers, sun signs, places of worship, calendars, any or all of these. But there is no known answer.

Positioning the Dolmens

OF course it is not known how many monuments were erected in Jersey but there is good reason to believe that there were many more than have survived to date and, even, that there are more to be discovered.

Even the ones that have survived have been affected, not only by natural causes but also by use of their stones in later buildings or by being cleared for farming.

There are certain features which seem to be constant in the positioning of monuments although exceptions can be found. The larger passage graves of the main Neolithic are generally on higher ground and have entrances facing more or less easterly. This is most likely in response to the sun's movements.

However, later monuments such as the known gallery graves or *allées couvertes* in the island are found on low lying land near the sea. Faced with so many uncertainties, the task of deciding exactly what they were used for remains extremely difficult. Perhaps it is advisable to take the advice of the late RE Education advisor on the Island, Derrick Best, who felt we should recognise and regard them as 'special places'.

This has led to many theories concerning the religious beliefs of the Neolithic people. Do these tombs indicate a belief in rebirth or do they reflect the miracle of life by being shaped like a pregnant woman? Or both? Or any other theory?

The continuing challenge of archaeology is to try and answer these questions in order to clarify the development of *Homo sapiens.*

Two of the menhirs (top and bottom) and the ossuary which can be found at Les Blanches Banques, St Brelade

Burying their Dead

ALL the tombs that have been discovered show evidence of entry or disturbance since they were originally sealed. It is difficult to judge, therefore, how the Neolithic people arranged the rites for their dead. What it is possible to assess is how they buried their dead.

While human bones have been found in many of the main monuments, the rituals associated with death in most cultures are so complicated that the very few Neolithic finds unearthed by archaeologists cannot justify more than the merest speculation concerning the way in which death was handled.

In some monuments dissociated bones have been found which are suggestive of scarification — exposure of the dead so that the flesh rots before the deposition of the bones in the grave.

In others and, sometimes in the same mound, for example at Les Monts Grantez, both dissociated bones and complete skeletons have been found.

In much later graves, for example in late Neolithic to Bronze Age chambers, there is some evidence for cremation. Of one thing, though, it is possible to be sure. That is that only specially selected bones of individuals were placed in the main monuments.

What happened to the rest of the population is unknown but the fact of selective burial would indicate that some of the people in the community were more important than others.

Whether or not these people were chiefs, or religious leaders, remains a mystery.

How Neolithic People lived

THE major difference between Neolithic people and their predecessors (known by archaeologists as Mesolithic people) was the introduction of food producing regimes, based on cultivating grain and domesticating animals compared to the former activities of hunting and gathering. The priority of the Neolithic people was to establish a community where farming could take place and extend outwards which involved cutting down forest, tilling land, cultivating crops and grazing cattle.

It is now thought that domestic structures would have been made of wood and covered in turf or thatch. In shape, they could have been round, rectangular or even trapezoidal. Modern preference, for this area, favours round houses although the replica at La Hougue Bie is rectangular. Utensils were made from clay, wood and stone.

For external work, they would have used flint axes and sickles and there is no doubt that they could make rope and utilise wood and stone.

Life within their homes would have been communal and there is good reason to believe that each community would live in a compound with a wooden palisade or raised earth rampart as defence against predators rather than as a defence against more aggressive neighbours. During the Neolithic Age, which ended with the introduction of bronze (made from tin and copper, and now categorised as the Bronze Age) skills in the manufacture of pottery and the grinding and polishing of stone tools developed greatly. Building skills also developed equally, the results being the menhirs and dolmens that have survived to this day.

We have no knowledge of their religious convictions nor of their structure of communal life.

However, there is good reason to believe that the dolmens were more than just tombs. They must have had both a religious and a community significance and would have been a focal point for certain communal activities. The amount of work that went into their construction must mean that they were of very special significance.

The Dolmens of Jersey

We hope that you have enjoyed this brief guide to the Neolithic stone monuments of Jersey. It is the first in a series of 'Welcome to' booklets that is planned to give our visitors an introduction to the many facets of history and natural history that are contained in our small but fascinating island.

It is worth repeating that this guide cannot nor does it intend to give any more than an introduction to the monuments. Those readers who would wish more information should visit the Lord Coutanche Library at the Société Jersiaise, the Jersey Museum or the museum at La Hougue Bie.

Peter Hunt 1997

Definition of the word 'dolmen'

In Brittany, structures of prehistoric age consisting of large, flat, unhewn stone resting horizontally on three or more stone structures are called dolmens. In Wales they are called 'cromlechs'.

This is, according to the Oxford English Dictionary, the correct use of the word 'dolmen'. Through popular usage, however, most graves and tombs made from stone by our Neolithic ancestors are referred to as dolmens.

In this guide, we have carried this populist usage though conscious that the term is popular and not exact. The exact term should be 'a Neolithic stone monument'.

Sources

The Dolmens of Jersey by Ian Kinnes and James Hibbes, La Haule Books, 1988. Jersey in Pre-History, Société Jersiase, 1976. Jersey in Pre-History, Barry Cunliffe, Société Jersiaise, 1995. The Neolithic Revolution, Sonia Cole, British Museum, 1970. Channel Island Churches, John McCormack, Phillimore, 1986. First Farmers in the Channel Islands, John Renouf and James Urry, Jersey Education Department, 1976. The Archaeology of Brittany, Normandy and the Channel Islands, B Bender with I Caillaud, Faber and Faber, 1986. Neolithic Communities in the Channel Islands, Mark Patton. British Archaeological Reports Series 240 pp 124, 1995. Lectures at La Hougue Bie, Doug Ford (of the Jersey Museums Service),1996.

Printed by Grange Press, Southwick, Sussex